AF575423

PLATED DINOS

Featuring *Stegosaurus*

BY JOSH ANDERSON

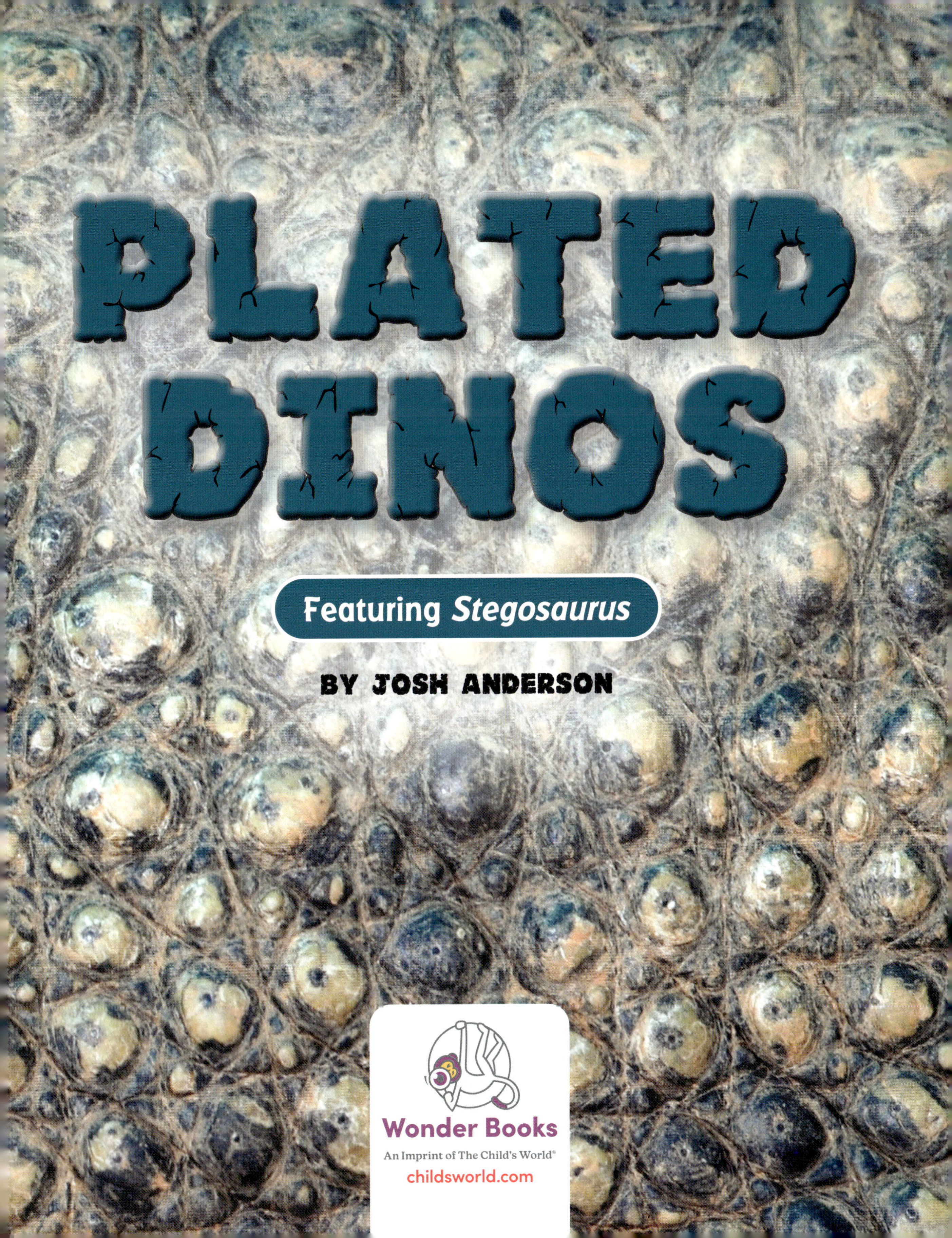

Wonder Books
An Imprint of The Child's World®
childsworld.com

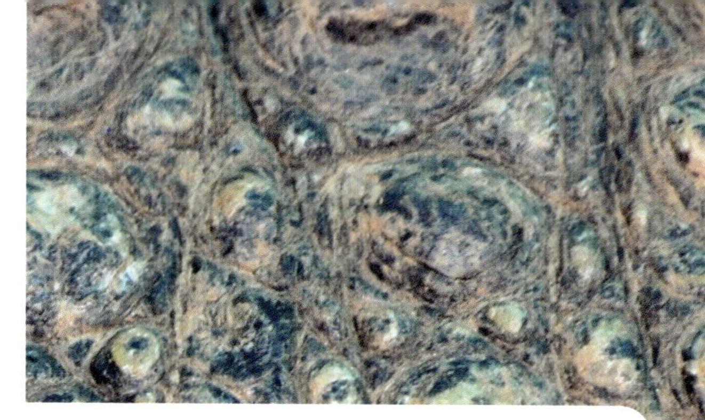

Published by The Child's World®
800-599-READ • www.childsworld.com

Photography Credits
Cover: ©Suwatwongkham / Getty Images; page 1: ©Pan Xunbin / Shutterstock; page 5: ©Warpaintcobra / Getty Images; page 6: ©Carl Court / Staff / Getty Images; page 9: ©Carl Court / Staff / Getty Images; page 10: ©MR1805 / Getty Images; page 12: ©Herschel Hoffmeyer / Shutterstock; page 13: ©Kitti Kahotong / Getty Images; page 14: ©Elena Duvernay/Stocktrek Images / Getty Images; page 15: ©Chainarong Boonyindee / Getty Images; page 16: ©Tuul & Bruno Morandi / Getty Images; page16: ©Julio Francisco; page 17: ©Julio Francisco; page 19: ©gorodenkoff / Getty Images; page 21: ©Daniel Eskridge / Shutterstock

ISBN Information
9781503865303 (Reinforced Library Binding)
9781503865921 (Portable Document Format)
9781503866768 (Online Multi-user eBook)
9781503867604 (Electronic Publication)

LCCN 2022940998

Printed in the United States of America

About the Author

Josh Anderson has published more than 50 books for children and young adults. His two sons, Leo and Dane, are the greatest joys in his life. Josh's hobbies include coaching youth basketball, no-holds-barred games of Exploding Kittens, reading, and family movie nights. His favorite dinosaur is a secret he'll never share!

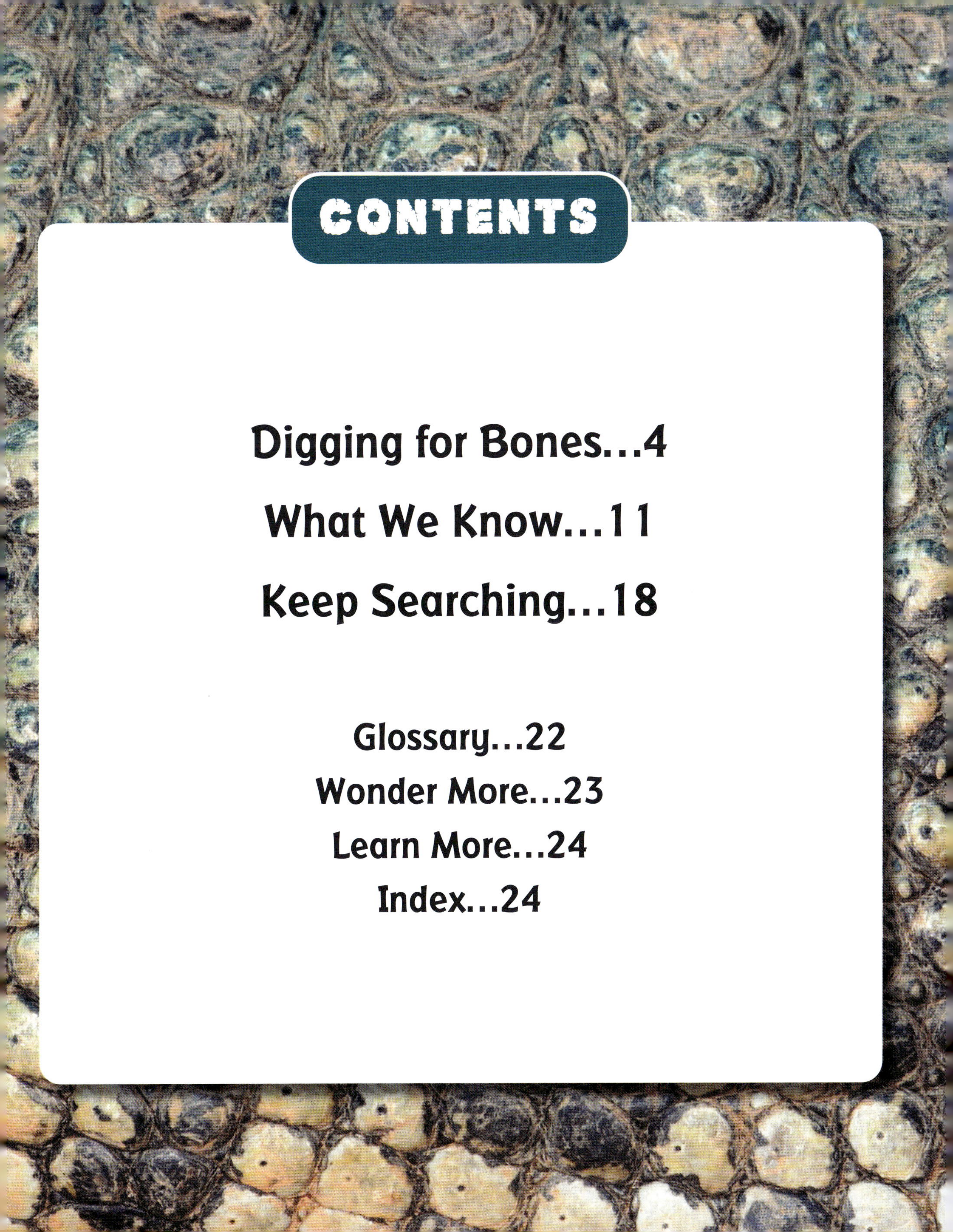

CONTENTS

CHAPTER 1

Digging for Bones

Pretend you can time travel to a prehistoric age. . . . You've gone back 155 million years. It is the late Jurassic period. You're in a forest in North America. A giant animal is standing nearby. It is eating from a bush. The creature is about the size of a school bus. It has huge plates sticking up on its back. This is *Stegosaurus* (steg-uh-SAWR-uss). You know *Stegosaurus* won't try to eat you. The dinosaur is a **herbivore**. You move closer. But then, you see something that stops you. *Stegosaurus* has four huge, sharp spikes on its tail. You back away slowly. One swing of that tail and you'd be in big trouble!

How do we know so much about a creature who lived long before the first humans? The simple answer: SCIENCE! Let's learn more!

Stegosaurus weighed more than a bulldozer.

This *Stegosaurus* skeleton was found in Wyoming. It is on display at the Natural History Museum in London, England. Its name is Sophie.

Humans have been studying *Stegosaurus* for almost 150 years. The first *Stegosaurus* bones were found in Colorado in 1876. They were sent to a famous **paleontologist** named Othniel Charles Marsh. At first, Marsh thought the bones belonged to a prehistoric turtle relative. Marsh named the creature *Stegosaurus*. The name means "roofed lizard."

Almost a **decade** later, a nearly complete *Stegosaurus* skeleton was found. It was also found in Colorado. It helped scientists see what *Stegosaurus* really looked like. In 1915, the skeleton was put on display for the public. You can still see it today at the Smithsonian Museum of Natural History in Washington, DC.

Only a few nearly complete *Stegosaurus* skeletons have been found. In 2003, one was found in Wyoming. The **specimen** had 19 plates on its back. It also included a skull. Many dinosaur skulls are crushed when they are found. But this skull was not broken. Scientists could learn more from it.

A dinosaur's skull can tell us about how strong its bite may have been. It can also help reveal what the creature ate. The *Stegosaurus* skull helped scientists learn how the dinosaur chewed its food. They found that *Stegosaurus* probably had cheeks. Scientists figured this out by looking at the shape and placement of its teeth. *Stegosaurus's* bite was not as strong as other herbivores. So its cheeks were helpful. They gave the dino more room to hold and chew its food many times before it swallowed.

Stegosaurus had a long, pointy head with a toothless beak at the end.

Scientists have compared *Stegosaurus*'s brain to that of a golden retriever.

CHAPTER 2

What We Know

Stegosaurus belonged to a group of dinosaurs called stegosaurs. Stegosaurs were herbivores. They walked on four legs. Stegosaurs had bony triangle-shaped plates along their backs and tails. They also had long, pointed spikes on the ends of their tails. *Stegosaurus* was the largest stegosaur.

When It Lived: 155 million years ago - The Late Jurassic Period

Where It Lived: In the forests of North America, Europe, Asia, Africa

First Discovered: 1876, Colorado

Stegosaurus had a short neck. It probably ate from plants and bushes low to the ground. Its diet may have included ferns, mosses, fruits, and **conifers**. Some scientists believe *Stegosaurus* lived in herds. The herds probably included dinos of different ages.

FUN FACTS

- The plates on a *Stegosaurus's* back were called scutes.
- *Stegosaurus's* brain was tiny. It was about the size of a walnut.
- The set of four spikes on a *Stegosaurus's* tail is called a thagomizer. This name comes from a comic called *The Far Side*.
- Some scientists think *Stegosaurus* swallowed rocks to help it digest the huge amount of plant matter it ate every day.
- Some scientists thought *Stegosaurus* had a second brain, located near its rear! But this has been proven to be false.

THEN AND NOW

The word *Stegosaurus* means "roofed lizard." Othniel Charles Marsh gave it that name because he thought the plates on the dino's back were flat. He thought the plates covered a *Stegosaurus's* back like the tiles on a house's roof. After another specimen was found, Marsh realized the scutes were actually placed **vertically** on the dino's back.

The plates on a *Stegosaurus's* back may have been flexible and contained many blood vessels.

The name *Miragaia* means "wonderful Earth goddess."

Stegosaurus wasn't the only plated dinosaur. Here are a couple of others from the ancient world:

Miragaia (mee-rah-GUY-uh) looked like a cross between a long-necked **saurapod** dinosaur and a stegosaur. *Miragaia* lived around the same time as *Stegosaurus*. Its bones have been found in Europe.

Chunkingosaurus (chung-king-oh-SAWR-uss) was much smaller than *Stegosaurus*. It had bony spikes on its shoulders. Its bones have been found in China. It lived around the same time as *Stegosaurus*.

UP FOR DEBATE

No one can say for sure exactly why stegosaurs had plates. They may have helped to protect against attacks. But some scientists think the plates could have helped with thermoregulation. This is how a creature keeps its body at a certain temperature. Maybe future discoveries will help scientists know for sure.

STEGOSAURUS

(steg-uh-SAWR-uss)

VS

Length: 29.5 feet (9 m)

Weight: 6,800 pounds (3,084 kilograms)

Top Speed: 5 miles (8 kilometers) per hour

Weakness: Weak bite; not very intelligent

Best Weapon or Defense: Tail spikes between 2 and 3 feet long (61 to 91 centimeters)

KENTROSAURUS

(ken-troh-SAWR-uss)

Length: 16 feet (5 m)

Weight: 3,598 pounds (1,632 kg)

Top Speed: 5 miles (8 km) per hour

Weakness: Smaller than *Stegosaurus*; also not very smart

Best Weapon or Defense: Could swing its spiked tail very hard (*Kentrosaurus* means "spiky lizard.")

CHAPTER 3

Keep Searching

Some scientists believe a strip of land once connected North America and Europe. It was like a bridge connecting the continents. It may have disappeared because ocean levels rose. The continents may have just drifted apart. And some people think the land strip never existed.

A 2007 dinosaur discovery may shed some light on the issue. A *Stegosaurus* **fossil** was found in Portugal. Portugal is a country in Europe. Many *Stegosaurus* bones have been found in North America. *Stegosaurus* would have needed the "land bridge" to get from one continent to the other. The discovery of the fossil in Portugal supports the idea that North America and Europe were once connected somehow.

New dinosaur fossils are discovered around the world every day.

A recent find in China helped scientists understand the link between stegosaurs and other armored dinosaurs. Most stegosaurs lived about 150 million years ago. This includes *Stegosaurus*.

In 2016, a stegosaur named *Bashanosaurus primitivus* (bah-shah-noh-SAWR-uss prih-muh-TEE-vuss) was found in China. *Bashanosaurus* lived 10 to 15 million years before most other stegosaurs. Many of its features are similar to dinos that lived before the stegosaurs. This helped scientists learn more about how stegosaurs **evolved** from their older relatives.

Scientists learn more about dinosaurs with every new discovery. Maybe YOU will be the next paleontologist to teach the world something new about these giants of the past.

While they all have unique qualities, all stegosaurs have a row of plates along their back.

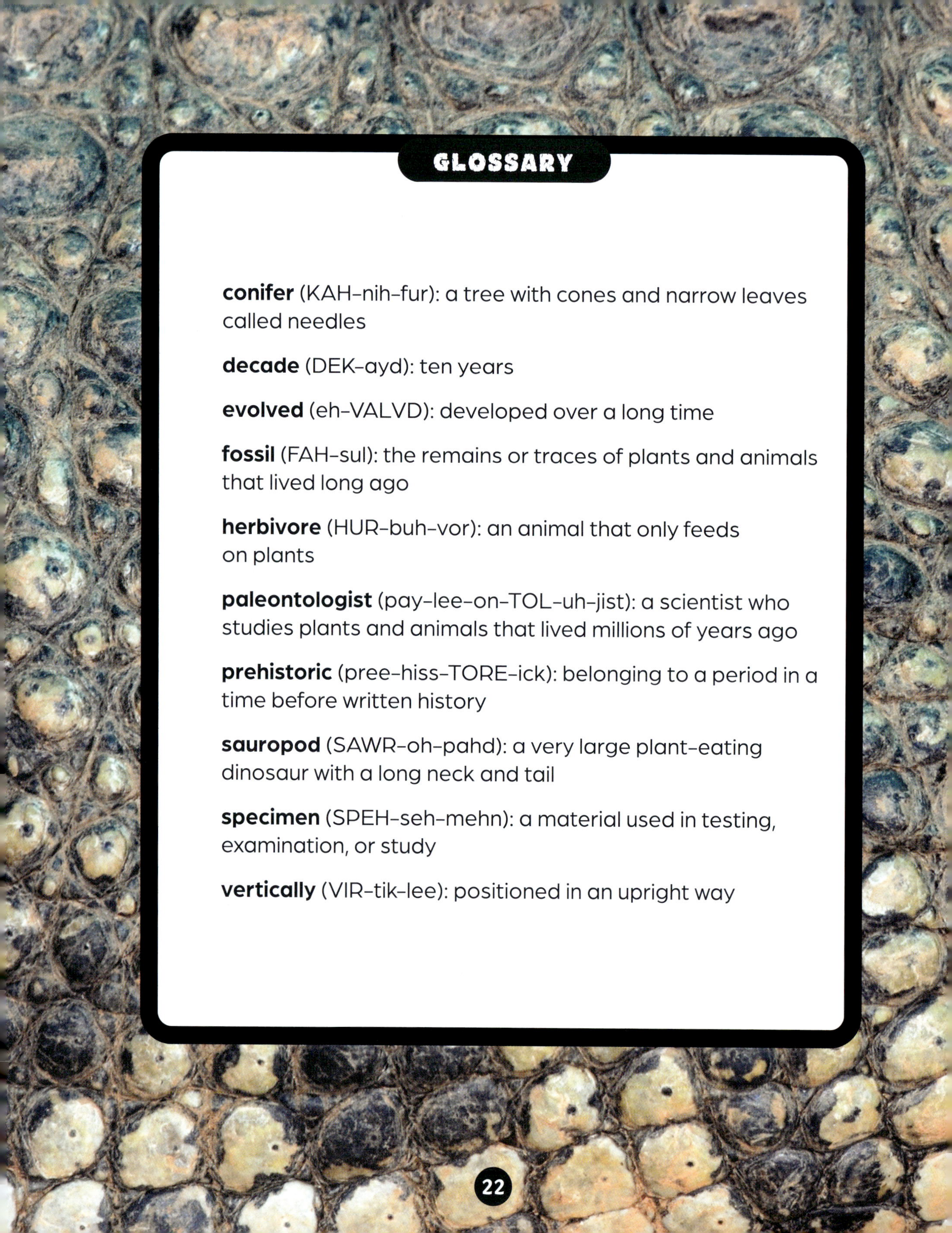

GLOSSARY

conifer (KAH-nih-fur): a tree with cones and narrow leaves called needles

decade (DEK-ayd): ten years

evolved (eh-VALVD): developed over a long time

fossil (FAH-sul): the remains or traces of plants and animals that lived long ago

herbivore (HUR-buh-vor): an animal that only feeds on plants

paleontologist (pay-lee-on-TOL-uh-jist): a scientist who studies plants and animals that lived millions of years ago

prehistoric (pree-hiss-TORE-ick): belonging to a period in a time before written history

sauropod (SAWR-oh-pahd): a very large plant-eating dinosaur with a long neck and tail

specimen (SPEH-seh-mehn): a material used in testing, examination, or study

vertically (VIR-tik-lee): positioned in an upright way

Think About It: Imagine your jaw and teeth were very weak, like *Stegosaurus*. How would it change the way you had to eat? What foods would you miss the most?

Talk About It: Ask your family or friends what kind of dinosaur they would choose to be. Would they want to be a fierce predator, like *T. rex*? Or a plated herbivore, like *Stegosaurus*? Or maybe a long-necked sauropod, like *Apatosaurus*?

Write About It: Imagine you woke up tomorrow with a long, spiky tail and huge plates running down your back. How would it change your life? Write a story about your first day in your new body.

MESOZOIC ERA

Triassic Period	Jurassic Period	Cretaceous Period
201–252 Million Years Ago	145–201 Million Years Ago	66–145 Million Years Ago

LEARN MORE

BOOKS

Carr, Aaron. *Stegosaurus*. New York: AV2, 2021.

Kelly, Erin Suzanne. *Dinosaurs*. New York: Children's Press, 2021.

Radley, Gail. *Stegosaurus*. Mankato, MN: Black Rabbit Books, 2021.

WEBSITES

Visit our website for links about *Stegosaurus*: **childsworld.com/links**

Note to Parents, Caregivers, Teachers, and Librarians: We routinely verify our web links to make sure they are safe and active sites. So encourage your readers to check them out!

INDEX